Steven Philip Johns

Time and Emotion

Best Wishes

Steven Philip Johns

The Fantastic State Publishing
Company Limited

17th August 2007.

This first edition published 1st May 2006
by
The Fantastic State Publishing Company Limited
The Loughborough Innovation Centre
Loughborough University
Epinal Way
Loughborough
Leicestershire
United Kingdom
LE11 3EH

Email: fspspj@btinternet.com

Printed and bound
by
Allsopps Limited
Nottingham
United Kingdom
NG3 1FH
All rights reserved.

ISBN 0-9552793-0-5

This book, I am certain, would have remained a dream had I not met and married Mary MacLeod.

Her amazing faith, support, understanding and advice, together with her valued editing skills have steered a random collection of jottings into this well ordered volume.

Time and Emotion, the book you hold in your hand, is the dream I have had throughout the last five years. Sharing my experiences of massive personal happenings that everyone on earth may have thrust upon them is manifest because of her.

From the bottom of my, now, happy heart,
Thank you Mary.

Foreword

Why did I write this book? I didn't, I thought it, lived it and spent time on Telendos in the summers of 2004 and 2005 and the Christmas holidays at home in 2005 to compile, edit and format it, finally finishing it in the last weekend of February 2006.

The experiences recalled here stem from a moment shared with my late wife, Beverley, in the summer of 2000. We heard a beautifully poignant song on the radio: 'I Hope You Dance' sung by Leanne Womack and written by Mark D. Sanders and Tia Sillers. Tears welled in my wife's eyes as she moved towards me to hug me. I think now that she knew then she may not live for much longer, and she wanted me to know that, when she had gone, it was okay for me to 'Dance' again when we could no longer be together.

The poems, as I dare to call them, started to appear in February 2001. At that time I was living in a fantastic emotional state. I have two excuses for this: I was very, very sad because my wife had died in the previous December and I had been introduced and become totally absorbed by a new friend I had met by complete coincidence only days after the funeral. I find it incredible to look back and imagine what my life and feelings were like then; up and down doesn't begin to describe. Someone told me around that time that it helps to write things down. I did this and very often a 'poem' popped out.

Between February and June of 2002 I attended a course of neuro-linguistic programming (NLP) in an attempt to learn more about what makes us think, feel and behave the way we do. More 'poems' popped out.

These last five years have been an amazing journey. I have formed some wonderful friendships and have learned how rich life can be. The most valuable, single lesson I have learned on this journey is this: be true to yourself first and foremost, live your life according to your values when you have discovered what they are. Some call these dreams.

Some of my dreams are here in this book.

If any of them play a chord in you I will have realised another dream, if not, write some of your own!

SPJ
On The Rocks Café, Telendos, Greece
20th July 2005,
Sileby, Leicestershire, United Kingdom,
25th February 2006.

Contents

Poems:-

Continued...

Contents continued

Poems continued:

'There is no truth.
There is only perception.'

Gustave Flaubert 1821 - 1880

In the beginning...

...they lived happily ever before.
On December 5th 2000 a wife angel died.
On December 9th she was buried.
The husband was very sad.
On this day a lonely angel telephoned the Husband. She had never met him.
Lonely Angel was lonely because her husband had died a while ago.

On December 11th the Husband met Lonely Angel.
They talked and talked all day. At the end of the day they danced.
Lonely Angel and the Husband thought they had fallen in love.
They certainly behaved that way.
For six months they had a fantastic time.

Upon the anniversary of Wife Angel's death the Husband laid flowers upon her grave. With red ribbon he tied a laminated card to the lovely flowers.The card had a picture of two dancers on the front which was painted by Jack Vettriano.
Alas, Lonely Angel and the Husband did not live happily ever after.
Lonely Angel misunderstood the Husband.
The Husband misunderstood Lonely Angel and himself.
They both tried very hard to understand.
Lonely Angel became very, very sad.
They left each other without saying goodbye.

Upon the second anniversary of Wife Angel's death, when the Husband visited her grave, he was very, very, very sad.

He lived in a pub.
He had a happy-sad Christmas in the pub.
From his bedroom window, up on the second floor of the old pub, he could see the little church on the hill which stood in the graveyard where Wife Angel was buried.
Whilst he lived in the pub he began to understand.
The Husband, on occasions, laughed and made friends here.
At the pub he was called "The Elder".

On June 28th 2003 The Elder said goodbye to his many new friends and moved to Scotland.
A Scottish angel had found him and made him happier.
But Scottish Angel could not be truly happy with The Elder although she did love him sometimes.
Upon the third anniversary of Wife Angel's death The Elder was neither happy nor sad.
He became Scottish Angel's "friend", had a quiet Christmas and said goodbye after New Year's Day.

On February 14th 2004 the "friend" moved back to his home town. He rented a big house and his teenage children came to live with him. He had left them many years before because he had fallen in love with Wife Angel.
They called him Dad.
Dad helped them to grow up.
The teenagers made Dad very happy by growing up.

On the 15th May 2004 Dad met a summer angel.
Dad made Summer Angel very, very happy.
Summer Angel understood Dad.
Dad understood himself.
Dad understood Summer Angel.
Dad became very, very, very happy.
They danced.
Upon the fourth anniversary Dad forgot to visit Wife Angel's grave.

On the 24th of September 2005 Dad married Summer Angel.

At 1pm on the 5th of December 2005, exactly 5 years to the minute since Wife Angel had passed away the Husband stood by the graveside of Wife Angel.
He was alone.
He said these words:
"Thank you for looking after me.
I have found true happiness again.
I hope you can rest now.
Goodbye my love."

On the gravestone, apart from the dates and Wife Angel's earthly name is a simple inscription which reads: "Love is Forever."

The laminated card, now faded and water sodden still has the ribbon tied to it, although it has turned grey now. After all the wind and ice and snow and rain and sunshine over the last years it is a wonderous thing the card remains there.

On the back of the card it gives the title of the picture as "Dance Me to the End of Love."

The hand written message, still just readable, says: "We Danced!"

Time's Dance

Time's dance dallies, dragging here, spinning there.
Pinball potent, flashing, ringing,
Bouncing, pinging.
Slow ticks, fast tocks;
Paradox.

It is not constant, no way.
Fill each bubble minute
With 'sixty seconds worth of distance run'
And it is gone,
As quick and silent as a thief.
A token smile may remain,
For your loss, your pain.
But idle away each passing day
And boredom's slothful clinging limpet
Slows down time almost to stop.
Lazy scum living past their allotted span.
Time...
It is so unfair.
No honour
In a contract with the con' man.

But know this and know this well:
Our last moment,
Last event,
Last second,
Last dying pulse of conscious thought
Will be myriadfold and everlasting.
This capsule awaits us all.
Waitless, weightless, tethered helium filled balloon of eternity.
Free from time at the last......
And in this place where there is no time
There is no enemy.
Grim Reaper is time's defeat.
Satan Time forbidden entry.
Here is complete beauty.
Time steals all beauty....
All.....except this.

The Last Time

I do not grieve.
I did not grieve.

I travelled today playing Pachelbel's 'Canon in D'
Over and over, time and time again, louder and louder.
Like a film's end just before the credits
Like a dam bursting, video on fast rewind
Memories in a minor key.

The last time I talked to her she was not there.
The last time I kissed her, oh so cold.
A stolen lock of her big burgundy hair.
All breath spent long before she was old.
The last drink was a tumbler of lime,
"Bliss, I am happy." Then sleep..
The last words, sense for the last time.
The last meal and a glass of wine.
The last time we danced she cried.
The last birthday.
The last holiday.
The last year.
Gone.

I do not grieve?
I did not grieve?
I know not grief!

I know sad.

I know black mood for I know not why.
Black, so black, a billion light years from light black.
So deep down dark words spoken cannot escape.
All falls in, imploding … no way out.
I do not grieve!
I did not grieve!

Then, Pachelbel in a minor key.
Unlocking?
I know grief. But it is not me.

Gabriel's Song

Time has taught me temperance in all things.
Except in love.
Love is selfish, urgent, stronger than I,
and all consuming.

Love I have in plenty and this will not die with me.
Time I have, here, now, only a little.
So I tread unselfish, thoughtful steps.
Doors slam on the options of my mortality.

Preparing the path to my infinite memory.
Letters written to soothe certain future pains
So they, case-shut damned certain, know
I will shine bright beacons for their new reality.

Mortal burdens soon to shed,
Not one will I leave behind.
Only love, the buildings of my life and my blessings.
That love, our love, she will take to another's bed.

This Fantastic State of Being

We talked into the night
And loved on to the morning;
Brightness grew in flashes.
Deep, dark sadness blossomed into light.

Leaping chasms of loss and gain.
Juxtaposed grief and joy.
Fighting mulched emotions,
Ecstasy builds on dead love's pain.

The embedded fissures of feeling
Churned to the surface.
They hurt like burst blisters
Before the start of healing.

Without motive, ambition or fear
I came to you that Monday.
I found truth and warmth
And the freedom to openly shed a tear.

Love and sadness ebb and flow
Dumping debris in tears and sighs
But new springs cleanse
With reality in love's afterglow.

I will love you into each night
And take you through to the morning;
This fantastic state of being, though
May burn too fast and bright.

Love is...(Part 1)

...not a light switch
You can turn off and on.

...blinding at first illumination
Delicious sensation,
Life bursting anew.

...adapting to make room
For gigantic plans;
Fusing by the second,
Evaporating viscous gloom.

...seeing through their eyes,
As though you were they.
Giving all and more
To a whim
That appears then fades away.

...childlike,
All innocent, safe and complete.
Yet danger lurks
Amidst amour
For death and deceit
Await unwary souls.

...dying to know you,
To take you to the end,
But bonds break
In the storm raged tide
Of misunderstanding and one sided fake.
Victims flounder like flotsam,
With no place to hide.

...at its end
With a bleeding heart
No surgeon can mend.

...not a light switch,
You can turn off and on.

...like a candle in the wind.
Protect from breeze and blame.
Or keep your tinder dry,
To re-ignite loves tender flame.

Love is…(Part 2)

...letting go
When you don't want to,
Or have to,
For the last time.
Inside,
You knew.
Bridges crumbling
Behind you.
Heart expelling
Love made,
Through tears,
Regrets and fears.
Naked understanding
No more.
Cocooning
Like spider's prey
In web bound confusion;
Love's stifled cry,
Let anger die.
Walk on.

For a time
There is no sense.
Let bygones by;
Somehow,
Find a way
Within your soul
For you,
To forgive you
And to say goodbye.

Love is...(Part 3)

...hell furious,
Like a woman's scorn.

When trust splits asunder,
Love born
Dies,

With super-nova cries
And split atom's thunder.
Fusion to fission...
"You told me lies!"

Eden to Armageddon.
No compromise.
"You'll tell me no more!"
Slammed locked door.
Loves blue-white passion

Explodes...
Spewing molten hate
"But I didn't mean..."
Like spit in a furnace
Unheard and unseen...
"Wish you'd never been!"

Why?
Look back beyond
The abysmal abyss
To that first kiss,
When eyes first met.
Was there deceit in this?

Probably!

Love is...(Part 4)

...hurting
When you leave.

Like angel's hands
Holding your heart
A little too hard.

But protecting from harm,
Treating equally
Tomorrow and eternity.

They carry you
'til you can love again.

Even if you grieve
Through a long refrain
Believe!

Your heart is in safe hands.

Love is...(Part 5)

...home,
If your heart is there.

It is not a house,
Not bricks and mortar,
Nor a place with hot water.

Not the street where
Little you
Grew
Strong and wise

However strong the ties.
It is not a town,
Nor a city,
Or an island in the sun.
(There's a pity!)

Home is knowing
As you near,
The smiling feeling
Which is all healing;
Open arms
And hugs a-plenty.

Never empty.
Home is safe
On solid ground,
Where your love
Is unbound
And is beyond compare.

It is your keepsakes' safe.

What really, really matters
In your world
Is there.

If this is not so,
Move!

Love is...(part 6)

...protecting
Your kids, your kin

From pain
And blame.

Stroking their hair
To show you care.

'There, there, there.'

Holding them
So close,
And tight
That only air
Can get in.

Fighting their fight
No matter
Who's right.

Taking chances,
Mending fences;
Fending off
Foes
And
Woes
With equal fire.

Standing between
Them and harm.
You in cold,
Them in warm.

When the fears have flown
Clean their wounds,
Dry their tears
And together
Share comfort foods.

In clean sheets
Tuck them.
They know,
You know,
Safety reigns
In their
Lion's lair.

Time for you?
You live to fight another day!
Pour a glass
Sit down
And with a well earned sigh you say...

'Kids! Who'd 'ave 'em, eh?!'

Love is...(Part 7)

...showing
How much
You care
By:
Giving,
Receiving,
Holding,
Having,
Laughing,
Wanting,
Telling,
Listening,
Creating,
Making,
Not faking,
Beaming,
Even gleaming,
But not gloating,
(too much),
Trying,
Not moaning,
Not lying,
But laying,
Relaxing,
Not stressing,
Supporting,
Not leaning,
Building,
Not breaking,
Fixing,
Sticking,
Mending,
Praising,
Not phasing,
Daring
Doing,
Risking,
But not all,
Kissing,
And not missing,

Wishing,
Hoping,
Sharing,
Being,
You.

But most of all
Living,
And,
Alas,
Dying.

Stream

Autumn leaves on meandering stream
Leave no trace, no ripple, no evidence
Of ever passing this way.
May never have lived or ever been.

What good now to bare and barren tree?
Deserted on breath of dank and mizzle wind,
To brave winter's slaughter naked and alone.
In frosted earth grasping, choking roots do plea.

Snared, broken, sodden, hopelessly defied
Storm torn branch, half submerged, damming
Relentless flow, catches leaf.
To comfort, chasten or to chide?

October's flood spews autumn's waste
Down drains and stream bursting dams
And banks in an hours gushing fury.
No love here in this season's tragic haste.

Earth now cleansed of feeble, once flamboyant leaves.
Depressed and lonesome tree sleeps near death.
Sapless in dark despair. Certified all but dead.
No pride nor beauty here where nothing grieves.

Even in desolate and withered hearts,
Life returns where love remains.
Chords ring out in major key.
Again, loves relentless rhythm starts.

Seeds sown in haste and hopes
Feed on last years fall.
Virgin spring to pregnant summer,
Life joins love and to autumn elopes.

Christmas Eve

A temple of comfort for lost souls, and found one's too.
Solace in drink?
No, in each other.
Drink shakes loose the trials and tribulations in heart and mind.

A throng one-fifty strong; loud and laughing.
Trouble and strife,
This is life.

A moment in time, travellers passing through.
Lights twinkle on tinsel; a score or more of points of view
Flash by in an instant.

Amidst the beat and bump of modern song
Behold and wonder the experience of mutual attraction,
Formed in a second and lasting a lifetime.

Make good from an old piece of wood
And rest your pint a while,
And breathe in this bristling humanity, generosity and equality....
And smile.

Move on enriched and understood.
A place has a purpose in your time.
Destiny only happens once my friend
Savour it while it lasts, each of your moments past
Were your destiny.

Cymbal of Symbolism

Each tinsel strand, bauble, band,
Coloured light, joyous sight,
Card posted, feast hosted,
Gift wrapped, afternoon napped,
Hand shaken, embrace taken,
Smile received, tale believed,
Cracker pulled, wine mulled.

All, now, in this old box refrain
'Til the cymbal sounds again.

Each life touched, plan hatched,
Deed done, race won,
Rule bent, pound spent,
Lesson learned, bridge burned,
Doubt killed, wish fulfilled,
Heart mended, friendship blended,
Seed sown, love grown,

Until next you hear the cymbal play,
And this old box sees light of day,
Where ever you choose your head to lay,
Your hopes and schemes
And gleaming dreams
Will help you find your special way.

New Beginning

Setting sail with no map or plotted course.
Dead, flat horizon for days on end.
Waking hours empty tacking to and fro'.
Sleep filled with what was and might have been.
Nightmares with casts of angry contemporaries blaming you.
Old friends now foe in these dreams of the awful new.

Then two capes come into view;
A smiling suitor and a new found friend.
Cynicism and suspicion, your only two trustees,
Advising to proceed with care in extreme,
Steer with equal water in between.

Stores empty, you run aground.
Desperate for succour and some faint reason,
Any rugged shore will now suffice.
Luck and fate on opposing sides of this dice,
Degrees of good and bad on the other four.

Bloodied, dazed and hungry you greet dry land.
Like souls offer respite and belonging.
Food and shelter is loaned to you.
Promises of rest and more
Extinguish fears of everlasting loneliness.

This is a time for taking.
Don't ask,
Your turn for giving is not now.

Slowly, life's reason grows again.
Plans become clearer as thoughts stop spinning;
A true friend is close now
And that sweet enticing honey
Of your new beginning.

On The Road Again

After so long
Marking time,
Life's rolling stone
Glances by,
Nudging me.
I join the flow,
No longer alone.
A piece of the whole
Paradoxically, free.
Playing my part.
Off I go
Into compelling tide.
Content to be
In society
Once more for all
No wish to hide.
My money
In my pocket
To save
Or fritter
On Champagne.
Striding to regain
My place here.
Plans abounding
And making sense.
Ages of pain
Fading fast.
Sunshine
Bursting through rain.
Full of futures
Past passed by
As I, yes, me!
Am on the road again.

Mirror

Who do you see?
You throw everything back at me.
I press my cheek to yours.
So hard and cold;
Thousands of years old,
Yet you only know what I know.
You stay, I go.

I return angry and you are too.
I open up my anger looking through
To the other side.
Peel an onion layer by layer;
When you're done nothing remains.
Except my tears,
And a hundred fears.

I undress before you
And you see nothing new.
I touch.
Hand on hand, kiss on kiss.
My love and soul you dismiss.
Diamond alone marks your face.
Unyielding, inert and commonplace.

Nothing do you keep.
Nought to reap.
Yet should I strike too quick
You break,
All fake.
Fragmented reality does not mend,
Misunderstandings that never end.

I close my tired, weary eyes
And slow but steadfast realise
Who I really am.
I dream of him who has to be;
Knowing fills every part of me.
All buried now, sins long past;
Mind and soul unlock at last.

Without You

When my life caved in
Half a year ago
Only you, only you
Kept hold.

So tenuous, so thin
Were the threads.
One snap more.
Gone.

Options disintegrated
Before my eyes,
Until only two.
Exist or die.

Bleeding and broken,
Last thread torn,
Your hand you gave.
I took.

Your story touched me.
Strength in humility.
Knowing by proxy.
Understood.

The power behind the phone.
Without you,
Now,
There'd be no me.

We jest now,
But many a truth
Is hidden there.
So take care.

A special place in me
For you.
Without you,
There'd be no now.

Dance

Two hearts, two bodies,
Two minds entwined.
This Dance,
Revered romance,
This parody,
Spine tingling melody;
Future never ending, yet,
One moment from now,
Too late.
This must have love,
Urgent breathless desire,
Fusion's fire.
All give.
All take.
No mercy in this love we make.
You give me you.
I give you me.
We take each other.
Burning passions,
Intimate sensations,
Unspoken secrets exposed
At our joining's summit.
Vacuums fill with sighs.
Alone no more.
Look into our eyes,
Truth sheds its disguise.
We lock our love
As lust subsides
In the aftermath's embrace.
And listen.......
The music still plays.

Lay You Down

When I lay you down in the evening,
And kiss your tender face,
You will look at me
With searing honesty
And, then, to our special place
We'll float like feathers falling,
Into union, into love.

Before me, you will slide into sleeping,
And I will listen to your peace.
In your comfort dreams that this will bring
I will softly stroke your hair
As you sigh your sweet safe song,
Your other selves
Will know I am always there.

When I am sure you are safe and sound
I will come to you.
In blissful slumber and ordered mind,
Keeping you at rest,
Protecting you from harm,
Tucking you into me, into warm.
My angel forever blessed.

As dawn's gentle light emerges through
Curtain cracks I will catch you
As you wake,
Lest you should fall too fast
Into our new day.
I will touch-start your heart
And soothe your loving ache.

Now we move into new morning,
I will dress you in fine linen,
Place gold around your neck
And kisses on your lips.
Your eyes shining heart rays.
Our dream complete
Until the end of all our days.

Moving on

June solstice day,
Rising sun horizon
Over bird song,
Beyond bursting green
Of trees,
New season's dawn exploding,
Hopes afore unseen.

Long days past
Shortening in my mind,
With these ecstatic
Dreams a-making.
Push and passion
Make happen
New life for the taking.

Real like fire
Consuming deadwood;
Ash remains
'Till first wind scatters.
Every glowing minute,
With a twist and turn,
Is all that matters.

Soon,
This book closes.
But at every break of day
I can wonder upon
The majesty
And the magic
Of moving on.

Opening

My heart, my soul, my mind, my feeling
My understanding,
My desire, my fire, my passion.
My future, my hope, my dream,
My love, my honesty, my truth,
My life.

Please take it all.
It is yours.

My plan, my vision, my ambition,
My skill, my tribulation,
My triumph, my glory,
My reputation,
My achievement, my testimony,
My tools, my invention,
My story, my work,
My all.

Do with it
What you will.

My voice, my song, my hearing,
My breath, my seeing,
My smell, my taste,
My haste,
My touch, my caress, my living
My yesterday, my tomorrow, my today
My forever.

All I ask in return
Is
You.

Eastern Promise

Light rising over eastern horizon.
Still dark autumn air causes no stir.
My world is safe in this delusion
Until the hour of Mammon's plunder.

Night leaves day all revealing
As tasks at hand slope into mind.
Plans afoot show their meaning,
Hope and purpose intertwined.

Reality fills my space of dreams
Whilst Monday morning blues emerge.
Freedom gives way to others schemes;
Hard shoulder in place of pillow-soft verge.

Minutes race where seconds strolled.
Weekend waltz now work-day jive.
Building bridges and growing old
In this bloodless coup of nine to five.

But, I loved and live to love again.
And pay day's flush of fortune
Of my making keeps me sane.
Eastern promise, it'll be Friday soon!

Shafts of Gold

Stuck.
Immovable, dogged, frustrating feelings.
Which way should I turn?
Unsatisfied in all my dealings.
Answers glaringly missing
To questions of simple truth.
Nothing obvious to me anymore
Like it was in my youth.
Complexities grow with age;
Wisdom not acquired without pain
It seems.
Show yourself, Sage!
Fill the unwritten page
With that which I do not know.
Love is not the answer;
Clouds of confusion,
Swirling illusion,
Mixed up emotion.
Distil!
Now.
Catalyse!
Before my eyes.
The smog evaporates
Revealing
Shafts of Gold,
Which light my understanding,
As I realise
The awesome beauty of compromise.

Absolute

I rack my brain, my deepest recess;
Search deep dark down
To the epicentre of me.
Further still into my soul,
To the smallest electron of my consciousness.

In this quest I am resolute.
I discard frail lust and fragile Mammon.
Sensation is drivel, pleasure minute
Compared to this:
The want which is absolute.

On my way I pass by ambition,
Recognition, promotion.
Even happiness trails in my wake,
Altruism, kindness and goodness sake
Far behind on my expedition.

Building a better world is for others care,
My self centre masked and shielded
This want to find for those who dare.
Go further still.
Go on, I am almost there.

There, that most elusive prize.
Last breath spent, no more disguise.
It is your love I want to take with me.
At my last, in your arms, your lips on mine,
Seeing through your eyes for all eternity.

Whispers

Listen to the whispers from your heart,
Not the shouts from your head.
Do this and you can be happy.
But it may seem like folly at the start.

Common sense abounds in mundanity.
Invention flows from the soul.
Your head brokers safe dealing,
Your heart wagers on uncertainty.

Art and genius thrive on passion,
Finding new ways to enrich humanity.
Pushing far beyond convention,
Spitting in the face of reason.

Look at a child shining
As it discovers something new.
Heart and mind speak as one
In a face prone to smiling.

Be the broker between your heart and mind,
Bring them together as friends.
Speak up heart and head quiet down!
And unknown wonders you may find.

Molehill Mountain

Pimple of brown earth
Upon glistening green,
Metaphored from birth.
Here, all the blind have been.

With tight shut eyes
In deep black dark,
This Everest defies
Wisdom's flashing spark.

Impossible ascent,
Worthless toil,
For a one-legged ant
Just circles in the soil.

Monsoon rain
Drowns kindling hope.
All pain no gain;
To death elope.

Earth seethes sucking mud,
A second more, too late.
Hear the coffin thud
With a thousand times your weight.

But, take wings
And see this from above.
'Tis why the nightingale sings
Of everlasting love.

The ant-awesome mountain,
From a different view,
Is nature's rich fountain
Where the blind can see too.

For Those Who Are Not Here

Absent friends
And past lovers and sisters
And dear departed mothers.

No time found to make amends.

In good time
Bad feelings fade,
All debts paid,
Duty served
And farewell bade.

Upon strong hearts peace depends.

What if?...

...or may have been,
No end scene,
Or cut off clean

In the middle meet loose ends.

Raise your glass,
Let bygones pass,
No regrets alas.

Let all around us hear
The resounding cheer.

For all, far and near,
Loud and clear,
A toast well meant....

...for those who are not here,
or are to heaven sent.

My Dad

I yam ded glad
That 'e is my dad.

Hey!
The fings 'e say
To mek each day
OK!

'e tort me
t' reely be
Me

Frew 'is eyes
The world's disguise
Was shed

And each night to bed
When I lay my 'ed
I say
Fanks
And no fear!

Coz,
Wi'out my dad
I wud be worse than dead;
I'd never 'ave been 'ere!

Robin

Many times,
Since last
We danced,
A robin
Visits me.
Hello,
Say I,
How are you?

Each time
He looks at me,
Chirps, hops
And flies away.

After
He calls
Amazing things
Come my way.

Once,
An old,
Dear friend,
Long years since
We'd shared
A smile,
Crossed
My path;
We made amends,
And laughed awhile.

On another day,
A new found friend
Grew fonder,
And so did I.

The day I left
An old house,
Glad to go,
Robin bade
Farewell.

I guessed
He'd stayed.

Until today;
A song played
On the radio
"I was lookin' for you."

Beyond my window
Outside,
On leaf lost tree,
Robin arrived.
He perched,
Hopped,
From branch to branch,
Chirped.
Danced?
For me?

Sad-Happy

Lots of love,
All kinds of love
For the one who now moves on.

From the moment you were born;
First talk,
First walk,
First friend,
First holiday by-the-sea.

Schools and rules,
Jobs and fools.

Go on,
Go well.
Time will tell.

Spare a spare thought for me,
Occasionally.

But, get on with life,
Your life.
It is your turn now.

Find a love that you can truly say
Is yours.
One that you make,
For you.

See the world,
Your world.
Bring into it
Who you choose.

Fight fair
And you'll never lose.

Remember you have choices,
Respect your inner voices.
Listen to them,
But question them,
For oft' they're from another's tongue
Less knowing than your own.

You know you
Better than all the rest.

Strive to be your best,
But, be happy.
It is your right.
And be sad when you need.

Both at once sometimes;
Like me now.
It does not confuse.

Sweet tears
For past years
And all those yet to come.

I Will Be Here

Hello Son,
I love you too,

It's just harder to say
(as your Dad)

Our society,
Our convention,
Our 'way of doing things',

I mean,
It ain't right, is it?
Or is it?

Yes it is!

Son!
Do what I should have done,
But didn't!
Do what I might have done,
But couldn't.

Don't hold back
Like I did.

In Nike style...
Just do it!

Play the field,
Find your space,
Be the ace,
Sow your oats
but....
Spare the gloats

Go on my Son
You can do it

I love you Son
Because.....
I do

Your generation
Knows more than me.

Like.....
Einstein said (of Newton)
"Standing on the shoulders
Of giants"

I am no giant.....
But,
Stand on my shoulders.....
My back is not
Yet bent.

Be you....,
Really you.

Don't hold back.
Go for
What you want.

Whilst I'm able
And our world
Is fairly stable,
I will be here.

Your time is now.

Go on Sam,
Say...
"This is what I am!"

Slow Boat to Catharsis

Fireglow light at Piraeus dawn,
Half a day or more to sailing time,
Waning gibbous moon looks down, forlorn,
Chased by sun, which will soon outshine.

Brightening light exposes shackled giants,
Jet powered, multi-coloured, floating mountains;
Archimedes laughs at our science,
Tethered by ancient anchor chains!

Hours amble slowly, dockside,
Saunter through shade to shade,
From Athen's searing sun must hide.
No cop-out from forty plus centigrade.

Time to think as departure delayed,
All holed up 'til dusk drowns light.
Ticket's void lest all dues paid.
At sunset 'Rodanthi' sails into this night.

A thousand dreams have passed,
Fey false signing this and that road.
Now, this end begins at last.
Morrow hails a brand new episode.

Ship sails through storms regardless
Of wind and night and calm.
Angels' watch over us is relentless.
To steer follyful heart from harm.

At first anchor day bursts in.
Roll off, roll on!
Bristling bustle, disembarkation din.
New life now, old day's gone.

Six ports on I stand on solid ground.
All sunk, those grieving years;
Been rocked and rolled and messed around,
Better now with no dead love's tears.

'Rodanthi' sails on to a new dawn day,
Full or empty off she goes.
I watch, smile and turn away.
"Take me taxi!" ...to where, who knows?

Shooting Star

You came here for the sunshine,
Or to pause a busy life,
Or to sit and be a part of
Your family, self or wife.

You found a friendly welcome
And peace in plenty assured.
New faces became friends
As the ouzo poured.

Wind or calm, the waves
Lap precious time ashore.
Embedded in your heart,
A yearn to return for more.

Many tongues are spoken
And many more understood.
The urge to be one with here
Leaks into the common good.

Soft echoes of your soul
Ascend on a midnight, clear.
Captured in a star
To return year on year on year.

So, before you leave this heaven
Look into our night black sky,
It will only take a moment
As an echo star shoots by.

The First Smile

Was it wind, or was that a smile?
Enter thus a tiny human's first attempt.
Deliberate act or happy accident?
If you let yourself believe in both,
A smile will form on your face.
You can't help it can you?
This smile shown to someone else
Compels them to duplicate it.
Then, damn it some one else is infected.
Two, four, eight, sixteen.
Before you know it the whole cave is smiling.
Oh dear now they have gone out into the Garden,
Made eye contact with Eve and you know the rest;
A little laugh and eyes averted.
This warmth is now spreading unabated.
There is no stopping this now.
Thirty-two, sixty-four, one-two-eight.
This is bad and way too late.
What can be done?
Absolutely nothing.
Just got to let it ride.
From this, you cannot hide.
Can this random act of smiling
Reach the warrior's door?
One thousand, two thousand, four.
Will Death Guard let it through?
He can't stop it.
The smiling majority have cast their vote.
Cynics among you please take note.
It will catch you when you least expect.
Go on, I dare you.
If the first ever smile was a happy accident,
It hasn't done too bad for us has it?
Come and join me…………

Summer in Mind

Thoughts of lovely lazy days,
Warm as soft winds blow,
Paths of dreams in golden rays,
Sure and steadfast as we go.

Cloudless skies of pastel blue,
Poppies in fields of flowing green,
Happy birdsong chirping through,
Often heard but seldom seen.

Give and take of guiltless love,
Morning drifting into afternoon,
All in time; no push nor shove,
No goodbyes, just , "See you soon."

So, when summer comes to mind,
I think of all this with you,
All warm and good and kind,
When first our love was new.

Wind of Dreams

No loneliness in this sleep, brushed by wisdom
Of all ages past;
Feasting in emotions lost in conscious souls.
This wind of dreams carries me high,
Above humdrum overloaded wakefulness.
Leading me to unselfish love's tender beauty,
Naked and warm, free at last.

Who shares these waters in which I bathe?
Is it she who took me first?
Nights filled with urgent sighs,
Days waiting, tomorrows fading, passion waning, pastures new.
Maybe. Faint, familiar image. I see now.
A page re-read and then understood,
Real act of love, just unrehearsed.

Warm and sweet wind, clean and fresh;
Young summer sunshine.
Scented meadows full of flowers. Soft cotton dress
Adorning running girl. Hurrying toward me.
She runs on. Away and out of sight.
Fleeting anguish 'if only' and 'what might have been?'
Beaujolais love is no vintage wine.

Then is now but no regrets. Feeling full of giving,
New love, bursting desire.
Adolescent energies binding old experienced hands.
Listen to the wind's soft song.
It blows every which way wherever you lay.
Lean back, submerge, be caressed, indulge.
Reason dowsing ambition's fire.

I awake smiling. Some of my dream remains.
All is light. Blue sky. No moon. Stars all gone.
In dreams truths are tried.
Verdicts pass over into wakenings.
All those in my dream are now in me
I am free to love and in love. Don't question it. No need.
Wind of dreams, sail me safely on.

In Autumn Fields
(to Cossington Mill)

Cartwheel furrows in muddy gateway,
Half holding rain from yesterday;
Boot splash deep.

Over stile into narrowing lane,
To path squeezed by fences
Of wood and wire.

Windless air, misty breath.
Lonesome cloud streak
Spectrum stretched by afternoon sun;

Could be the infra-end
Of a summer rainbow.

Munching cows take
Plenty no notice
At our trespass.

Dog uneasy crossing stream
By bridge cobbled
Out of a dozen slippery sleepers,
Stolen from a bygone railway age.

Golden leaves hold
Now too feeble,
Fall
With each robin's landing call.

Leaf soft carpet mulches
In a week or so.

Then into open autumn fields,
Left fallow by subsidy,
Bankruptcy
Or environmental decree.

Whatever...
Nature wins!

Dog bounds unbound,
Chasing shadows
In wilting stubble.

White sun sinks to orange
Screened by trees
A quarter mile west.

Heron guards mill pools,
Statuesque.

Time to turn about
As dusk douses daylight.

But dog knows best.

"Pub's open!"
Obedient now.

The American

Ask not from whence I came
But to where I go.

Yes, 'twas fortune that I sought
And maybe a little fame.

I found though,
I could be bought
For others' dreams
Much grander than my own.
Gigantic schemes.
Streets with numbers, not names,
Dead straight and long.
Accents forged
From a hundred foriegn tongues.
Sunshine and bitter rain.
Cities that never sleep.
Horizon fields to sow
and many more to reap.

I work for worth and gain
To pay back what I owe,
Putting a little by,
The rest I send back home,
To my lady overseas.

I made guns and cars,
Broke rocks in mines,
Seen death of man by man,
And God.

I had to work,
And I did through foul and fair,
And now I have a store.
I just knew
My life, my lot
Was worth so much more.

Tomorrow,
My lady and my kin
From Ellis Island come.
I'll show them how I've done,
And what I've built,
And that
I am an American.

21 Steps to Heaven

Learn to learn
And keep learning.

Yearn to earn
And keep earning.

Look and see.

Touch and feel.

Seek and discover
The key
To be
The real you.

Listen and learn.

Keep close those dear.

Love.

Be loved.

Travel light,

Enjoy the journey.
The end is not arriving,
But a new beginning.

Own your own actions,

And your emotions.

Do right
For you
And others.

Be right
For you
And others.

Let anothers view
Come to you.

Understand
The learning of loss.

Share your gains
Be kind.

Say what you mean.

Follow your dream.

Accept this;
It is OK to find
That heaven,
Your three times seven,
May only exist
In your mind.

9/11 Re-Frame

Picture this:
A spaceperson dropped in yesterday.
Humanoid in form but rather over curious for the norm.
A small mill town near Leeds, England,
right on the High Street.
Garbed in white multi-layered linen and flip-flops,
no-one noticed her.
Local time 13.45.

She meandered through the smattering of earthlings
peering into shop windows.
She paused by a news stand and absorbed information.
She dare not touch the primitive media, for it looked so fragile.
"9/11 One Year On"

What could this mean?
So significant, so reverent, so much feeling.
She could taste the sincerity of this collective emotion.
Curiosity aroused far beyond safety for her, she set off in a search
for answers.

Sun shining down made pleasant this little backwater of human
endeavour.
Another media temple; this time shiny polycarbons.
She dared to touch.
Looking through racks she came to:
"Indi Rock" 911
She scanned it.
This could not be it. Too puerile. Too simple.
Of little or no meaning. Toooo LOUD!
Even humans would not revere this trivia.

On she bounded into a foot wrap bazaar.
There on a shelf, just above her eye line,
"Men's Sizes 9 – 11."
No, NO, she stamped, humans would not mourn feet!

Outside again, in the lovely sunshine, she was halted abruptly,
On the edge of a travelling way.

Savage roar of primitive un-refined machine squealed by,
selfish and crude.
Metal badge on rear end "Porsche 911",
Surely, humans would mark this one's demise with mild glee?

Into temple of knowledge she glided,
gathering bravado from each passing moment.
Sitting with aged, gruntled humanoids she stole a flimsy coloured
carbon pulp picture cache.
"NYFD- call 911 if you need our help"
Coloured images of big, red machine with ladders amidst
mountains of catastrophe processed in her brain.
Feeling truth trickle in she searched for better media.
Sounds and moving visions will fulfil.

In domed temple of avarice lit by wasted energy, transmitting
boxes offered completion of quest.
A beautiful and highly evolved female human gave answer.

"Today marks the beginning of reason. There is a better way at
the front line of conflict. Peace Direct offers support to those who
wish to prevent war and can do something about it. Do not think
you are too small to make a difference. As the Dalai Lama said,
'Try sharing a bed with a mosquito'.
Today we begin to make a better world, 9/11/2002."

She made a permanent note of this wonderful lady's name -
Doctor Scilla Ellworthy.

She had done her mission for this day.
Translated, her transmission to her mother ship went something
like this:

"Earthlings OK. In better shape than our last visit in 1002.
Not so sure about the music though."

Notes

Time's Dance: Page 12
The phenomenon called time is a perception. For a one year old child, one year is an entire lifetime. For a fifty year old it is one fiftieth of a life time. The longer we live the faster time seems to pass, unless boredom infects us. Does it stop at the moment of death? Maybe, maybe not.

The Last Time: Page 13
Music unlocks emotions. Convention and political correctness often shackle our feelings, or at least the freedom to display them openly. For me, my pent up emotions can flow if I play good music, loud and alone.

Gabriel's Song: Page 14
This poem is a tribute to a man I have never met. I was privileged to read the last letter he wrote before he died. The letter was to his beloved wife. I deeply respect his dignity, bravery, honesty and ability to face the truth.

This Fantastic State of Being: Page 15
I should have been certified as insane! In a normal, everyday context, with the simultaneous display of opposite emotions such as these, a fair diagnosis would be schizophrenia and manic depression!

Love is...Parts 1 to 7: Page 16 to 24
Love has many parts. There are many types of love. The residue of an affair of love takes many forms. I have made a start on a few of these aspects, as it seemed to me. I hope I live long enough to write of many more.

Stream: Page 26
On a dismal, cold, wet, awful autumn day when life is not going well it is as easy as sliding down a muddy bank to feel hopeless. Somehow, though, hope springs back to mind and a grain of positivity saves the day, even if it is still raining outside.

Christmas Eve: Page 28
I had the pleasure and opportunity of being an onlooker in a busy town pub on a Christmas Eve. The joy and togetherness evident was truly amazing.

Cymbal of Symbolism: Page 29
When the festive season ends and everything has to be put away again I find poignant reflection inevitable.

New Beginning: Page 30
There are many stories written about how hardship has to be faced before life can begin again. It is almost a rule of nature. It did feel as though I had no control over events, and that I was in the hands of fate.

On The Road Again: Page 31
Resolve kicked in the instant I realised I was really skint. I got a new job and knuckled down to earning some real money. It is amazing how so much else seems to fall into place when sensibility is restored.

Mirror: Page 32
To help another we have to be in a more resourceful state than they are themselves. The safety demonstration carried out before every commercial passenger flight in the world instructs us, in the case of an emergency, that we securely fasten our own oxygen mask before attempting to help others. We can't help anyone else if we are dead! We can't help anyone else in their self esteem if our own is low. Mine was when I wrote this. I don't think I helped much.

Without You: Page 33
I do not know where I would be now had I not met Ali. We became friends from a distance. There were times when I really could not see any future for me at all. She showed me that the future is all around. She encouraged me to write. We are still distant friends.

Dance: Page 34
OK. I admit it. This is a metaphor for having the best sex you can ever have. So what? It is amazing how good the fantasy can seem when one has abstained for a while!

Lay You Down: Page 36
The fantasy continues!

Moving On: Page 37
I woke up early on mid-summer morning and I watched the sun rise over the churchyard. I had made plans to move out of my second floor bedsit in the pub and I was fantastically excited. The very act of moving on is, in itself, sensational…. when you are leaving little behind.

Opening: Page 38
No! This was not a promissary note to my boss. This was what I wanted to say to the person I wished to spend the rest of my life with. I just hadn't found her yet.

Eastern Promise: Page 39
A little later on that year I had the good fortune to enjoy some lovely weekends. Seven day weekends ought to be an option for everyone. Alas, Mammon needs attention so Monday comes too soon.

Shafts of Gold: Page 40
The fantasy ran into a wall the size of the Hoover Dam! At times like these compromise is usually the best way forward. Sometimes, the compromise can seem like a bright light being turned on to show the way.

Absolute: Page 41
Back on track with a comfortable compromise the fantasised promissary note is given another airing and edit. Would I be happy with the decisions I have made thus far when I draw my last breath? Not sure. Maybe my memory will not be so good then!

Whispers: Page 42
I am told, by reliable sources, that there is a little voice in everyone's head. For me it is not always a *little* voice. But I do have soft whispers with big feelings from my heart. When I bring these two together I often achieve a happy result. Whispers is an attempt to share this.

Molehill Mountain: Page 43
To an ant a molehill is a mountain. To a single minded person who will not change their point of view a small irritation can become an enormous divide. I have experienced this. I have been, (still am) on one side of such a divide. I can climb down, but often I am not met by anyone at the bottom. So I fly and see it from above!

For Those Who Are Not Here: Page 44
I wrote this as part of what I was going to say at my wedding. I wished to remember those who had not come. Some had deliberately refused and I was sad. Of course there were others who could not be there.
I shortened this to 'absent friends' in my speech.

My Dad: Page 46
I have a picture, it is printed in this book, of me as a small boy wearing a cowboy suit. I gave this poem to my father on a recent birthday. It is written as if I were still 4 years old, with a bit of the last 48 years of experience thrown in.

Robin: Page 48
Very often, since Beverley died, an amazing event is preceeded by the appearance of a Robin. My level head tells me that this is just coincidence, synchronlcity at best. My other head likes a better explanation. Through the eyes of birds, angels watch over us?

Sad Happy: Page 50
It is wonderful to witness your offspring growing up. It is comforting to know they are becoming independant. It is a perfect opportunity to tell them a few pearls of wisdom at this time, because, for a brief moment or two they will listen. I wrote this for Emily, my daughter, at the point when we were to go our separate ways, residence-wise that is.

I Will Be Here: Page 52
In our civilised society it does seem to be very hard for a father to tell his son that he loves him. Even the odd hug is difficult. But it is a wonderful feeling to show, even if afterwards, all you get is a mumbled, stifled and embarrassed "Ok Dad!"

Slow Boat to Catharsis: Page 54
The first time I went on my own to Telendos I travelled from Athens port on a big, old ferry boat. The trip took more than a day, and was the most amazing journey I have yet experienced.

Shooting Star: Page 56
This poem adorns one wall in a little café/restaurant/taverna on Telendos, a very small island in the Aegean. I like to feel that I belong, for a week or two every year, to Telendos. I would love every good person on earth to enjoy this little paradise, but don't all come at once when I am there!

The First Smile: Page 57
I performed this piece in front of 120 associates at an end of course party. Ever since they have hailed me as 'Smiley Steve'. A few months after this I didn't smile much at all. Although I smile a lot again now I would like to be known as something else in future.

Summer in Mind: Page 58
Mary and I enjoyed a lovely first summer getting to know each other. Every day the sun shone. It was always warm and all around us was happiness. Apparently, we learnt later, it was one of the wettest summers on record!

Wind of Dreams: Page 59
When I am set to thinking as to how I arrived (survived) to where I am now, I often think of the friends and lovers with whom I have shared some of this journey. I am prepared to admit that a lot of what happened was wrong. But in every relationship I have ever had, a lot of it was right, very right! Maybe just the time was wrong?

In Autumn Fields (To Cossington Mill): Page 60
Although Cossington Mill is clearly signposted and marked on the map it does not exist anymore. This makes for several very interesting, elongated walks across open fields, because it is impossible to find. Tigger, our dog, likes this very much.

The American: Page 62
My paternal Grandfather stowed away on a freight boat to Canada, crossed Lake Michigan and settled in Detroit in 1924, leaving his wife and two young daughters in Cornwall. The tin mines had gone bust and there was no other work. I visited Ellis Island Immigration Museum in 2005 and absorbed some of the feeling my Grandmother felt when she joined him two years later. She had to stay on Ellis Island for three days with her two young daughters whilst her papers were verified.

21 Steps to Heaven: Page 64
I wrote this one whilst lazing on Paradise Beach, Telendos, on July 13th 2005. Tough job, I know, but someone has to do it!
Back to Gustav Flaubert here. Heaven is a metaphor. It does not exist, except in the mind. There is no truth, only perception. Time is perception. Time, therefore, must be heaven. Time I have, and so do you, so you and I are in heaven! Dream on!

9/11 Re-frame: Page 66
It was the first anniversary of 9/11 and I had Johnny Walker's five o'clock show on my car radio. His guest inspired me to write this piece. Officially, hijacked American Airlines flight 11 crashed into the North Tower of the World Trade Centre in Lower Manhattan at 08.46 Eastern Standard Time. Look at the picture of the clock on the front cover of this book (see picture notes on page 77). The minute hand, had it not been bent would be pointing to eleven minutes to nine. Also look where the second hand is pointing. Is it entirely subjective that there are so many 9/11s? Maybe it's just me!

Dedications

Time's Dance: Page 12
To Pauline Stanley - The clock you gave to me ticks constantly and eternally.

The Last Time: Page 13
To Beverley - To dance is to love. Love is forever. Sleep tight my love.

Gabriel's Song: Page 14
To CF - I never met you...or did I?

This Fantastic State of Being: Page 15
To Sally - I couldn't believe it. I still don't!

Love is...(Part 1): Page 16
To me - I learned so much from getting things wrong.

Love is...(Part 2): Page 18
To Annie - You taught me how to let go.

Love is...(Part 3): Page 19
To compassionate, even handed, divorce lawyers everywhere - Do they exist?

Love is...(Part 4): Page 20
To my Mum - Who I have left so many times.

Love is...(Part 5): Page 21
To George Wimpey et al - What a perfect home you built for us.

Love is...(Part 6): Page 22
Doreen (Dean) Anderson - Thank you for being there for them. God rest your soul.

Love is...(Part 7): Page 24
To all who feel that they have lost in love - Love is never futile.

Stream: Page 26
To Dr. Veronica Wilkie - Understanding and truth. No bull.

Christmas Eve: Page 28
To Tim Radley. What a memorable Christmas!

Cymbal of Symbolism: Page 29
To Janis and Wendy, my two sisters - So different from each other, yet together complete.

New Beginning: Page 30
To Richard Ward (Tricky) - An old hand at beginning anew. We taught each other much.

On The Road Again: Page 31
To Joseph Jaconelli - Thank you for the ride.

Mirror: Page 32
To Annie - When I looked at you I saw a lot of me.

Without You: Page 33
To Ali - Thank you for being there for me.

Dance: Page 34
To true lovers, everywhere.

Lay You Down: Page 36
To true lovers everywhere. Afterwards!

Moving On: Page 37
To Paul - Ironic, for one who always stays put, with feet firmly on solid ground, he is the first there to help when I am moving on. Thanks brother.

Opening: Page 38
To Mary - I had come to think that it was not possible again.

Eastern Promise: Page 39
To Mary - What a promise you keep and keep and keep.

Shafts of Gold: Page 40
To my workmates - Keep your dreams alive.

Absolute: Page 41
To Mary - My want which is absolute.

Whispers: Page 42
To Peter Hobson - A friend, coach, adventurer and writer. Passion and reason in equal measure.

Molehill Mountain: Page 43
To those who cannot forgive - Take wings and see this from above.

For Those Who Are Not Here: Page 44
To Evelyn Hewes - Almost as soon as you knew, you left. Upon strong hearts peace depends.

My Dad: Page 46
To Dad - Say n'more.

Robin: Page 48
To Beverley - Diamond glint in snow - swift uplifting rush - quiet bird in flight.

Sad Happy: Page 50
To Emily - A daughter dear. 'How much did you say you needed?'

I Will Be Here: Page 52
To Sam - Go for it son!

Slow Boat to Catharsis: Page 54
To Ian McDermott - A brilliant teacher, the coaches' coach!

Shooting Star: Page 56
To George, Poppi and Savas Trikilis - The custodians of my heaven on earth.

The First Smile: Page 57
To my NLP friends everywhere - Never stop smiling.

Summer in Mind: Page 58
To Mary - To seek life eternal is folly, but our summer can last forever.

Wind of Dreams: Page 59
To young lovers everywhere - It really can get better than this!

In Autumn Fields (To Cossington Mill): Page 60
To Tigger - Ever eager to be unleashed.

The American: Page 62
To Herbert Johns - My Grandfather. From Cornwall to Canada to Detroit to Cornwall to Nottingham.

21 Steps to Heaven: Page 64
To you, who read this book - Because you have, my heaven becomes just a little more real.

9/11 Re-frame: Page 66
To Johnny Walker - To my mind, the best radio show presenter in British Broadcasting. Travelling home without you will not seem the same.

The pictures...

Front Cover: 'Time & Emotion'
This is a photograph of a desk clock that was found in the debris after the collapse of the twin towers in September 2001. It stopped at exactly the moment of impact of the first aircraft. One infinitesimally small fraction of a moment that gave rise to billions upon billions of emotions.

Page 4:
Me, the author, hard at it under extremely adverse conditions at 'On The Rocks' Café/Restaurant in July 2004 on the Island of Telendos, Greece.

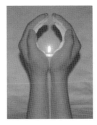

Page 17: 'Protecting From Breeze & Blame'
Mary and I spent a lovely weekend in St Ives, Cambridgeshire in September 2005. There is a brilliant little shop in the main street adjacent to Oliver Cromwell's Statue, called 'Metamorphosis'. This tea light holder, moulded out of what appears to be cement fitted this poem perfectly.

Page 25: 'The Other Side of Love'
New York is a truly amazing city. Around every corner there is something at which to gasp. On our last day there, after watching the Mayor's parade, making our way back to the hotel to pick our bags we bumped into this work of modern pop art. 'Love' stands on the corner of 55th Street and the Avenue of the Americas. Robert Indiana (Clark) sculptured his first one in 1966 and the image has appeared on 330 million postage stamps, millions of cards as well as this book!

Page 27: 'Bare & Barren Tree'
On Sunday 18th December 2005 in the bitter cold Mary, Tigger and I came across the bare and barren tree, standing alone half way up Beacon Hill in Charnwood forest. Waiting for love's relentless rhythm, no doubt!

Page 28: 'The Hop Pole'
40 Friar Street, Droitwich Spa, Worcestershire.
The original print of 'Christmas Eve' still hangs on
a wall in the lounge here in a clip art frame I
bought from Wilkinson's hardware store.

`Page 29: 'Bauble'
As we entered St. Peter's Square, during my first visit to
Rome in February 2006, workmen were dismantling the
Christmas tree. There were a couple of dozen by-standers
watching the goings on. Some of the baubles were given out
to people in the small crowd. Mary and I are now the proud
owners of one of Pope Benedict XVI's balls!
(I didn't know until I arrived home that Mary's reflection is on
the picture! Just left of centre.)

Page 35: 'Fusion's Fire'
I would like to say that I have searched the world over to find
this picture. It was beginning to feel like it! Whilst we were in
New York in September 2005 we found a brochure which led
us to this sculpture that stands in Central Park outside the
Delacorte open air theatre. I took 41 shots to get this one. The
passers by on that beautiful sunny afternoon must have
thought we were a little mad. But, hey, it was New York! The
sculpture has been there since 1977 and is made from bronze
by Milton Hebald.

Page 37:
The windows to my second floor attic room in the old pub. I
used to gaze out of these at the church on the hill and
wonder about moving on.

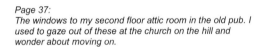

Page 39: 'Promise'
I stood on top of a little church on Kalymnos (the main
island adjacent to Telendos) to get this picture of the sun
setting over Telendos. I was glad they were not holding a
service whilst I was there! The Greeks take their religion
very seriously, and would probably have ex-communicated
parts of me had I been caught!
Thankfully, my friend Stuart kept watch.

Page 45: 'Absent Friends'
Every flower in this Wedgwood vase I picked from our
garden in Droitwich on a summer day in 2001. Every
plant that I picked the flowers from had been planted by
Beverley.
She lives on in that garden. These flowers in this pose
live on in an engraving on her headstone.

Page 47: 'The Cowboy'
This picture was taken with a 'Box-Brownie' camera
sometime around my 4th birthday in 1957.

Page 49: 'Robin'
On our way back to the car from the walk up Beacon
Hill on the 18th of December Robin appeared and
danced for us.

Page 55:
I bought this ticket at 3.45 a.m.Greek
time in Piraeus port. The number written
on it is the number of my first class
cabin.
I am very glad I hadn't economised and
booked 3rd. Class!

Page 56:
This is George Trikilis's business card which
he gave to me on my first visit to Telendos
more than 10 years ago. Beverley and I had
some wonderful holidays there.

Page 63: 'The American'
This is a picture of my Grandfather, Herbert Johns, taken
around 1925/26 in Detroit, USA.

End cover:
Minnack Theatre, Porthcurno, Cornwall, September
2004.

Emails to the author:
fspspj@btinternet.com

Time & Emotion by Steven Philip Johns
Available from all good bookshops
&
www.amazon

ISBN 0-9552793-0-5